Girlfriends
Gratitude

Journal

"Everybody has a story.
What's yours?"

—Kate Delaney

Girlfriends Gratitude Journal

Published by Tullamore Publishing

First Edition
Printed in the USA

ISBN: 978-0-578-80300-5

Girlfriends
Gratitude
Journal

TULLAMORE
PUBLISHING

Dallas, Texas

"Fill these pages with
Happy Thoughts,
Good Times and
Big Successes!"

—*Kathleen Delaney*

"Believe in the Beauty
of your dreams."

—Eleanor Roosevelt

"Don't allow other people to dim your shine because they are blinded. Tell them to put on some sunglasses."

—Lady Gaga

"Friendship is a gift
you share
with another friend."

—Jaki Baskow

"I never dreamed about
success.
I worked for it."

—*Estée Lauder*

"There is nothing like
a really loyal, dependable,
good friend. Nothing."

—Jennifer Aniston

♥♥

"Be Kind."

—*Ella Baskow*

♥♥

_____

_____

_____

_____

_____

_____

_____

_____

_____

_____

_____

_____

_____

_____

_____

_____

_____

_____

_____

_____

_____

_____ ❤❤

"Real friends never slip
through the cracks
in your life."

—Kate Delaney

"I always believed
that one woman's success
can only help
another woman's success."

—*Gloria Vanderbilt*

♥♥

♥♥

"A good friend
is like a four-leaf clover:
hard to find
and lucky to have."

—Irish Proverb

"Friends are like Jewelry.
They're precious gems."

—Vilma Söderman

♥♥

"Lots of people want to ride with you in the limo, but what you want is someone who will take the bus with you when it breaks down."

—Oprah

"Good friends are like stars.
You don't always see them,
but you know they are there."

—*Anonymous*

♥♥

There is nothing like introducing a friend to another friend and sharing the gift of friendship. We met in Las Vegas and discovered we both grew up in Cherry Hill, New Jersey. May your friendship grow like ours.

—*Jaki Baskow and Kate Delaney*

www.ingramcontent.com/pod-product-compliance
Lightning Source LLC
Chambersburg PA
CBHW030514100426
42813CB00001B/39